# Steyning Sc:

GW00472646

## Secrets of a Sussex marke. ..

*to Elaine,*
*with best wishes,*
*Janet Pennington*

by

Janet Pennington

**S.B. Publications**

First edition printed in 2007 by Janet Pennington
Reprinted and revised in 2009 by Janet Pennington
Email: jpsussex@hotmail.com

or c/o Steyning Museum, Church Street, Steyning,
West Sussex BN44 3YB    Tel: 01903 813333

This research is dedicated to Joyce Sleight of Steyning

Joyce taught several generations of children at Steyning Grammar
School to whom she passed on her enthusiasm for history in its many
guises. We met in 1978 during a snowstorm and since then, as friends
and research colleagues, not a day has gone by without some aspect of
Steyning's history, scandalous or otherwise, as part of it.

ISBN 978-0-9555703-1-5

This edition designed by E.H. Graphics, East Sussex Tel: 01273 515527.
Published by S. B. Publications, Seaford, 14 Bishopstone Road, Seaford, East Sussex
Tel: 01323 893498   Email: sbpublications@tiscali.co.uk

# List of Illustrations

The cover illustrations are taken from a map of Wiston and Steyning dated 1639, by Henrie Bigg, courtesy of *West Sussex Record Office, Wiston MS. 5591.*

The front cover shows St. Andrew's Church, Steyning (note the steeple) and possibly Gatewick House (top centre). There is also a general view of part of the High Street.

The back cover shows the north-west end of the High Street, with the road now called St. George's Place on the lower left, Mouse Lane on the far left, with H = the Rose and Crown alehouse – now the Star Inn. Please note that the houses are not accurately represented.

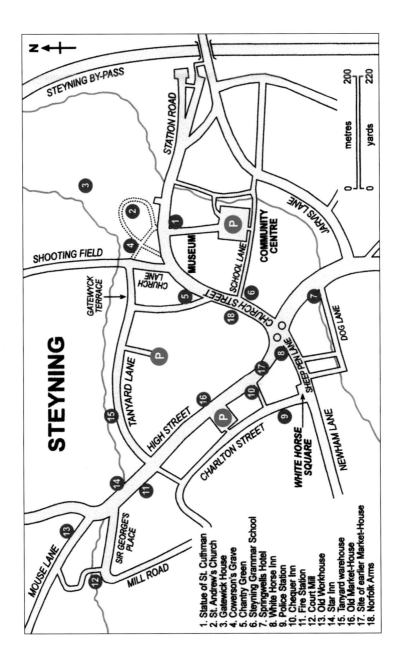

STEYNING

1. Statue of St. Cuthman
2. St. Andrew's Church
3. Gatewick House
4. Cowerson's Grave
5. Chantry Green
6. Steyning Grammar School
7. Springwells Hotel
8. White Horse Inn
9. Police Station
10. Chequer Inn
11. Fire Station
12. Court Mill
13. Old Workhouse
14. Star Inn
15. Tanyard warehouse
16. Old Market-House
17. Site of earlier Market-House
18. Norfolk Arms

# Steyning Scandals
## Secrets of a Sussex market town 1547-1947

### Foreword

This is a walking (or reading) trail for those interested in the scandalous history of Steyning, a medieval market town in West Sussex, situated under the north scarp of the South Downs, to the west of the river Adur.

Steyning has medieval timber-framed houses, a Norman church, a Jacobean Grammar School in a Tudor building (which has flowed out to a secondary site, becoming a large Comprehensive School), a defunct railway (1861-1966), Edwardian villas, Victorian houses, so-called 'artisan' dwellings and 20th century council and privately owned housing, plus 21st century infilling. There is a thriving High Street, a new Health Centre, an excellent Museum and Library, a Community Centre, churches and meeting venues for the various societies that flourish in the town.

Two chalk streams encircle the early town site, and the water used to run at least two mills, a tanyard and two breweries in Steyning's industrial past. The closing of the railway in 1966 meant that Steyning has not become a 'commuter town' but has continued to be a good mix of the young, families and retired people. Brighton and Worthing are within reasonable reach by bus or car. The coast and downland provides a wonderful network of cycle tracks, footpaths and bridleways, while the chalk, sandstone and clay soils produce mixed farming, good oak trees and attractive flora and fauna.

So – a good place in which to work and live, or to visit – but what of the promised scandals? The following pages are based on more than thirty years' research into Steyning's history. For those with an interest in source materials, footnotes and a bibliography provide the evidence for everything that appears in the following pages.

Any local scandal that has ensued after 1947 (just after World War II) will not be revealed in these pages. Perhaps it should be asked whether yesterday's scandal is today's entertainment? Scandal from four centuries ago can seem amusing today, but the participants may have been under sentence of death for their behaviour, which, with changing moral and other values, would not cause more than a short prison sentence or a ripple in a local newspaper nowadays. If readers feel that research on accidental death, adultery, assault, bestiality, black magic, butchery (of meat – vegetarians could be alarmed by this), drunkeness, imprisonment, libel, martyrdom, references to sexuality of whatever kind, smuggling and suicide from 1547-1947 will be upsetting, do not turn the pages of this book. You have been warned. No libel actions are to be pursued...

*Acknowledgements:* I would like to thank Joyce Sleight, long-time friend, research colleague and resident of Steyning, and Len Warner, Steyning solicitor, for their advice and encouragement. Writing about scandals is a little different from talking about them. Sue Rowland has kindly drawn a map of Steyning (p.iv) showing some of the places mentioned in the text as well as all the roads involved in walking the route. There is no excuse for being scandalously lost.

*Chris Tod, Curator of Steyning Museum, and David Thompson of Burgess Hill, have both contributed in many ways to this research over the years, though not, I am pleased to say, to the scandals contained herein. A few typographical errors have been corrected for this edition and an index for People and Places has been added.*

*Janet Pennington, Steyning, 2009*

# Steyning Scandals

## Secrets of a Sussex market town 1547-1947

Fig. 1. The church of St. Andrew & St. Cuthman, Steyning

In 1880 rambler and writer Louis Jennings caused Steyning inhabitants to consider a libel action. He noted that:-

Steyning is a very good example of a Sussex town – clean, neat, and old-fashioned, but sunk into a sleep as profound as that which fell upon the hero of the Kaatskill Mountains [i.e. Rip Van Winkle] after he had drank freely from the mysterious keg of liquor. A shop or two may be seen here and there, but the wares exhibited in the windows are such as have long gone out of date. Occasionally one of the inhabitants may be seen in the streets... looking [for] any neighbour with whom he may exchange a few musty ideas... One almost

1

expects to see a fine green moss all over an inhabitant of Steyning. One day as I passed through the town I saw a man painting a new sign over a shop, a proceeding which so aroused my curiosity that I stood for a minute or two to look on. The painter filled in one letter, gave a huge yawn, looked up and down two or three times as if he had lost something, and finally descended from his perch and disappeared. Five weeks later I passed that way again, and it is a fact that the same man was at work on the same sign. Perhaps when the reader takes the walk I am about to recommend...that sign will be finished...but I doubt it. There is plenty of time for everything in Steyning.[1]

Jennings obviously did <u>not</u> visit Steyning on market day, and no doubt used some poetic licence in his description. He was nearly in big trouble, however, as when the book was published, there was talk of libel action by the town elders. They were furious about the fine green moss…

Twenty two years later, in 1902, Steyning sounded rather more lively, as its short-lived newspaper, *The Steyning Observer,* (published at Orwell Cottage, 22 High Street) provided details of what was going on in December of that year.[2] The Christmas Fat Stock Show was on and there would be a Sale and a Dinner. The Hockey Club was busy, there were organ recitals at St. Andrew's Church, dances, a lecture on poultry keeping, a hypnotism demonstration, while at the Norfolk Arms in Church Street The Pongites, members of the ping-pong club (the

---

[1] L. Jennings, *Rambles Among the Hills,* (1880), 184-5
[2] C. A. Grigg, *Memories of Steyning,* (1967), 11

2

founders of the Steyning Walking Races – first held in 1903)[3] were meeting regularly.

Alas, by 1909, the fine green moss had descended again, or so it sounds:-

> Steyning...here we have another of the quaint, old-world little towns...which have the air of having gone to sleep somewhere in the Middle Ages. The railway seems quite irrelevant in so medieval looking a place, and discreetly keeps well to the east of the houses. Steyning is little more than a quiet village.[4]

Then in the same year:-

> There appears to be a lack of entertainments in Steyning...I was attracted to a group of about twenty persons standing on the kerb...I expected a street accident at least, but on going to ascertain the cause of this assembly, I found that the crowd was merely amusing itself by watching a passing cyclist inflate a tyre of his machine.[5]

So, let us take a walk through Steyning and see what can be found by way of a scandalous past - something that might be rather more interesting that a cyclist pumping up his tyres – a man with a wheelbarrow perhaps?

---

[3] I. Ivatt, *The Race,* (2003), 12
[4] F. G. Brabant, *Rambles in Sussex,* (1922, 2nd edn), 124, 127. (The first edition was published in 1909).
[5] A. Beckett, *Spirit of the Downs,* (1909), 172-173

We can begin at the entrance to Fletcher's Croft car park, near the Community Centre and opposite the church of St. Andrew and St. Cuthman. A rededication of the church took place on St. Cuthman's day, 8th February 2009, adding his name to that of St. Andrew. A statue of Steyning's very own saint shows him looking thoughtfully across the road to the church porch.

Fig. 2. St. Cuthman of Steyning, without his wheelbarrow, by Penny Reeve.

A booklet about the story of St. Cuthman is usually on sale at the Museum.[6] St. Cuthman, a shepherd, is said to have arrived at Steyning in the 8th or 9th century from Chidham, near Bosham, in the far south-west of Sussex. His father had died, so he placed his invalid mother in a one-wheeled barrow and set out on a journey to the east. He was an early Christian and wished to spread God's message.

The rope helping to take the weight on his shoulders from the handles of the wheelbarrow (basically an invalid carriage), broke after some miles, and his mother tumbled out. Some haymakers laughed at Cuthman's predicament, whereupon he called down curses upon their heads, and the rain immediately fell and ruined their work.

He made a new rope, of elder withies, and continued on his way. When his home-made rope broke for the second time, he had reached what was to become Steyning, and Cuthman wisely decided to settle at this pleasant spot. He built a timber church, later replaced by one of the finest Norman churches in the county.[7]

The church lies close to Steyning's two streams, the one to the north-west the source of power for mills and a tannery. The leather industry has made an important contribution to Steyning's history. Breach's Tanyard closed in 1941, but in the 1920s it was a busy place, as will be seen below.

---

[6] J. Pennington, *St. Cuthman of Steyning: A Journey Through Time,* (1993 reprint); a more recent booklet by G. Cockman, *Cuthman and a continuing tradition,* (2005), is a good read.
[7] J. Blair, 'Saint Cuthman, Steyning and Bosham', **Sussex Archaeological Collections** (hereafter **SAC**), 135, (1997), 173-92.

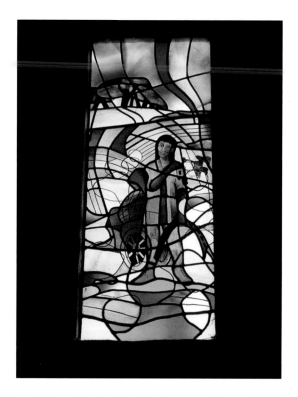

Fig. 3. St. Cuthman, his mother in the wheelbarrow, sheep and Chanctonbury Ring on the South Downs. The 20th century church window, by Alison Bolton, is in St. Cuthman's Chapel. Cuthman is holding the broken support rope to the barrow.

In the 1920s author R. Thurston Hopkins came to look at the tanyard, which in the early 19th century moved from the south-east end of the town to what is still called Tanyard Lane at the north-west end. The tanyard did not close until 1941 and was a busy place. Hopkins was speaking to one of the workers:-

> How old is that wheelbarrow?' I asked, pointing to a very ancient-looking vehicle. 'Old – very old', he

6

replied. 'It came from Lewes about forty years ago, and it was worm-eaten with age then. It must be e'en - a'most on a hundred year old'. 'P'r'aps it's the very barrow in which Saint Cuthman wheeled his paralysed mother when he came eastwards to build his timber church at Steyning,' I suggested. 'Don't know nothing 't-al-'bout that', said the man non-committally, 'but I heard that years ago they wheeled old Maria Digweed home in it after she had celebrated her eighty-first birthday at the "Rising Sun" [at Upper Beeding].'[8]

So, leaving such an undignified scene, let us walk through the churchyard, round the church in an anti-clockwise direction, pausing to the east of the porch to look up at the corbel table. This is the line of stones, many of them carved heads, that look down upon us below the roof eaves.

Close to,[9] or through binoculars, it is possible to see that the last head on the west, the second stone to the right of the downpipe, is a female with a headdress and she is holding her tongue, or the edge of her mouth. She has been described as 'the only silent woman in the parish'.[10] The other heads are of beasts or non-humans, and all are grimacing or looking very unpleasant. They are a warning against evil, keeping bad thoughts and evil spirits away from the church. The corbel table on the north side of the church is blank.

---

[8] R, Thurston Hopkins, *Sussex Pilgrimages,* (1927), 35-36
[9] The author climbed the church tower scaffolding to examine the female head some years ago.
[10] Grigg, 14

Fig. 4. The corbel table on the south side of St. Andrew's Church. The female mouth-or tongue-holder is the second stone to the right of the downpipe.

The woman's tongue- or mouth-holding harks back to an earlier time. It is difficult to put oneself into the medieval mind, but carvings in churches and cathedrals warning against sexual misdemeanours used to be common throughout the land. Most have been expunged, either during more puritanical times, or by church ministers who did not want their parishioners seeing explicit sexual scenes. These types of carving survive in abundance in the rest of Europe, particularly in Ireland, France and Spain. The carving on Steyning church seems to be warning against sexual sin, the oral cavity replacing and suggesting another. If you wish to follow up this subject in more detail, a great deal of scholarly research has been undertaken, especially by architectural historians Weir and Jerman. Their book *Images of Lust: Sexual Carvings on Medieval Churches* contains some eye-popping illustrations.[11]

---

[11] A. Weir & J. Jerman, *Images of Lust: Sexual Carvings on Medieval Churches,* (1986); J. Pennington, 'An 'Image of Lust' on Steyning Church?', **SAC, 129,** (1991), 251-2

8

Walk round to the north of the church, where Gatewick House can be seen.

Fig. 5. Gatewick House. Note the fine beech tree. Steyning's former harbour was in this area.

Once one of the several manors that made up the town of Steyning, Gatewick and its lands was owned for many years during the 16th and 17th centuries by the Farnefold family.[12] A Coroner's Inquest shows that James Farnefold was in trouble over 400 years ago, in 1547. The Inquest was held on 12th November of the year that Edward VI, the short-lived son of Henry VIII, came to the English throne. The County

---

[12] W. Powell Breach, 'Farnefold of Steyning', **SAC, 59,** (1918), 84-112

Coroner had called a jury and 13 men came to the court room at West Tarring.[13]

The murder of William Horley of Wappingthorn (an estate to the north west of Steyning) was discussed. The jurors heard that about 8pm on 10th October 1547 Horley, who was a servant of John Leeds Esquire, the owner of 'Wappingthorn in Steyning', was in a field there called the North Leed, with other servants of his employer. James a Barowe, a shoemaker of Henfield, Thomas George and Gerard White, both labourers, and Thomas Savery, a glover, all of Henfield, were with Edward Smith, a husbandman, and James Farnefold, gentleman, both of Steyning.

This mixed group, no doubt led by Farnefold of Gatewick, a neighbour of Leeds of Wappingthorn (their lands adjoined), came 'armed and riotously assembled there, killed 2 of his rabbits worth 4d. with 'hayse' [i.e. long nets], nets and 'pursenettes' [bag-shaped nets] and assaulted Horley and other of Leeds's servants, six of whom are named. This may have had something to do with rabbit warrens belonging to Leeds or Farnefold. Rabbits were 'farmed' and carefully husbanded. Their meat and fur were valuable assets to any landowner. The use of nets probably indicates that the rabbits were in an artificial warren or 'pillow mound'.[14]

Barowe was holding a bow and arrow and he 'shot and murdered Horley, giving him a wound with the arrow in the left side to the heart of which he immediately died'. Barowe immediately fled,

---

[13] R. F. Hunnisett, (ed.), 'Sussex Coroners' Inquests 1485-558', **Sussex Record Society** (hereafter **SRS**), **74,** (1984-85), xliii, 39-40. The number of men on a Coroner's jury ranged from 12 to 24.

[14] See T. Williamson, *The Archaeology of Rabbit Warrens,* (Shire Archaeology, 2006)

unsurprisingly, and disappeared. They were lucky, in that after White and George (later described as a yeoman or a tailor) spent some time in prison, all, including Farnefold but except Barowe, were pardoned, probably by the general pardon granted by Edward VI.

Barowe was arrested at Henfield on 18th October, eight days after murdering Horley. He escaped and fled, finally appearing nearly a year later in the King's Bench when he pleaded not guilty. A London merchant, a gentleman and a saddler all stood bail for Barowe, as well as an innkeeper at St. Giles in the Fields.

Finally, two years after the original crime, Barowe was acquitted of the murder, but his goods and chattels, worth £3 (about £300 today)[15] were forfeit. He was lucky to get away with his life and freedom and it is probable that James Farnefold had put in a good word for him.

There is obviously much more here than meets the eye, and it is possible that Farnefold was making a case for land ownership, or perhaps a rabbit warren, with his neighbour John Leeds of Wappingthorn. The murder was no doubt unplanned, except perhaps for that of the rabbits. Their fate is not discussed.

Walk on up the slope then turn right and make your way down to the rear entrance of the churchyard, but stop at the second tombstone of the row of four on the right. This marks the grave of William Cowerson who died in 1832.

---

[15] All valuation comparisons are taken from *Equivalent Contemporary Values of the Pound: A Historical Series 1270-2001,* Bank of England (2002).

Fig. 6. Group of tombstones including that of William Cowerson (centre).

He was a 31 year old Steyning stonemason and around the time of his death was working on West Tarring church. A known smuggling gang operated from this coastal village, and it is possible that the view from the church tower was useful in seeing when certain ships were approaching the shore. One has to imagine the shoreline rather further out than the present-day Worthing promenade. Cowerson was part of the well-organised smuggling operations that went on around these parts. They were usually backed by apparently respectable local businessmen and farmers. Cowerson could hope to make as much money in one night than he might in a year as a stonemason. He was a batman to the gang, which meant that he brought up the rearguard with a stout 6ft ash pole or 'bat', ready to knock out anyone's brains if they attempted to stop the smuggling run.[16]

It was a moonlit night when, at 3 a.m. on 22nd February 1832, a large gang of smugglers began to unload some 300 tubs of spirits (known as ankers – holding 10 gallons, or half-ankers, of 5 gallons' capacity, two per man, roped together and strung across the shoulders). They were moved through the Steyne and up the High Street – Worthing was quite a small town then – heading north for the crossing of the Teville Brook where the railway now runs. The old footpath is still there and can be followed to Broadwater church, where various routes lead over the Downs to Steyning.

The stream was quite an obstacle, and a footbridge caused a delay so the gang was momentarily halted. In the meantime the Coastguards had called the Preventative Officers, but possibly not enough bribes had been paid. Money frequently changed hands in order to allow smuggling runs to take place. Nobody crept about in imaginary tunnels under ground - the gangs were bold and ruthless and everyone looked the other way, including, often, the authorities. Lieutenant Henderson, armed with a gun, fought with Cowerson who broke his right arm with his ash stave. Henderson, desperate or ambidextrous, managed to get his gun into his left hand and fired, shooting Cowerson dead. The gang fled, some of the smugglers were captured, as were many of the tubs, and Cowerson's body was, depending on various sources, either taken

---

[16] See M. Waugh, *Smuggling in Kent and Sussex 1700-1840*, (1998, revised and updated), for more details about smuggling in Sussex and how it was organised.

13

to Steyning and back, or directly to the cool cellar of the Anchor Inn, now the Jack Horner public house, between the High Street and Lyndhurst Road, Worthing. The Coroner's Inquest was held there. Steyning's Parish Register, Burials for February 1832, lists William Cowerson as 'shot by Excise Officers' and it has been noted that the baptism of a William Cowerson, son of Maria White, singlewoman, took place on 3rd July 1831, presumably Cowerson's illegitimate son [17]

In the meantime the local newspapers made a meal of the story. Cowerson's name was printed as Cowardson (no doubt on purpose) and Steyning inhabitants were very angry about this. Their man, by now a local hero, was being done down.

Some of the liquor escaped capture and in due course a fine headstone appeared in Steyning churchyard, perhaps paid for by local subscription or any proceeds of the smuggling run. It is difficult to read the verse now, as the lettering needs infilling and clearing, but the stone is inscribed as follows:-

> Death with his dart did pierce my heart
> When I was in my prime.
> Grieve not for me my dearest friends
> For it was God's appointed time.
>
> Our life hangs by a single thread
> Which soon is cut and we are dead.
> Therefore repent, make no delay,
> For in my bloom I was call'd away.

---

[17] West Sussex Record Office (hereafter WSRO), PAR 183/2/23

He was certainly 'call'd away' – the penultimate smuggler to be shot in Sussex! It is said that he was a tall man, because of the length of his grave. It is a fine stone but a sad story.

Fig. 7. William Cowerson's gravestone in St. Andrew's churchyard, Steyning.

Cowerson's fate can perhaps be compared with that of another smuggler whose gravestone at Patcham church, now in the northern suburbs of Brighton, is 'Sacred to the memory of Daniel Scales, who was unfortunately shot on Thursday Evening, Nov. 7, 1796.' It reads:-

Alas! swift flew the fatal lead
Which pierced through the young man's head,
He instant fell, resigned his breath,
And closed his languid eyes in death.
All ye who do this stone draw near,
Oh! pray let fall the pitying tear.
From the sad instance may we all
Prepare to meet Jehovah's call.

Scales was a desperate smuggler, heavily laden with booty and was shot through the head 'only as a means of preventing a similar fate befalling his slayer'.[18] Smuggling was not a romantic or picturesque occupation.

Leave the churchyard by the northern entrance, and cross the road with care, noting the stream on your north – you can walk above the grating and see it rushing under the road to the vanished water mill that was part of the Gatewick Estate until 1878. Walk a little way along Tanyard Lane, until halfway past Gatewyck Terrace on the right, then cross the road and walk up an unnamed lane. This emerges at Chantry Green, now part of the garden of Chantry Green House, where on 23rd July 1555, Protestant John Launder, aged 25, a farm labourer from Godstone in Surrey, was burnt at the stake. This terrible fate befell 41 Protestant martyrs in Sussex during the reign of Catholic Queen Mary (1553-1558), 17 of them in Lewes.

John Launder had come to Brighton with a friend, Thomas Iveson (or Everson), a carpenter, in October 1554. They visited the home of Derrick (or Deryk) Carver, a beer brewer who had the Black Lion

---

[18] E. V. Lucas, *Highways and Byways in Sussex,* (1904), 199

16

brewery in the old part of Brighton. Black Lion Street can still be seen in The Lanes area of the town. When worshipping at Carver's house, all three were arrested by deputy sheriff Sir Edward Gage of Firle.

Fig. 8. Chantry Green House, which now includes Chantry Green, on the right, as part of its garden.

Launder was taken to Newgate Prison where he remained for seven months. The Bishop of London, Bishop Bonner, had him taken to his own house on 8th June and gave him every opportunity to change his mind about his Protestant views. He would not have to go to the stake if he recanted. Launder said he thought that confession to a Priest was unnecessary, and that at Communion the bread and wine did <u>not</u> transform and said 'I will never go from these answers as long as I live'. He was given a day to think it all over, then, as he refused to recant, at St. Paul's Diocesan Court in London he was condemned to death by burning.

Fig. 9. Chantry Green where John Launder was burnt in 1555.

This fate also befell Carver, who was burnt at Lewes, and Iveson, who was burnt in the precincts of Chichester cathedral. Steyning was chosen for Launder. Presumably these were towns where such an example needed to be made. The horrible scene can be imagined at Chantry Green, the memories passed on down the generations. It was in sight of the church, and as the dissolution of the chantries had begun on Easter Day in 1548, the burning happened only seven years later, and the Catholic authorities would have been making a religious and political statement when choosing the sites.[19] A plaque of remembrance

---

[19] J. Pennington, 'Documentary Evidence' in M. Bennell, 'New evidence for Saxo-Norman settlement at Chantry Green House, Steyning, West Sussex, 1989', **SAC, 138,** (2000), 226-227. The chantry priests would have lived near the church, but the actual business of the priests would have taken place at an altar in the parish church.

18

is situated by the steps to Steyning Museum just a little way down Church Street towards St. Andrew's Church.

Opposite Chantry Green, between 35 and 51 Church Street, is the spot where the only bomb to fall on Steyning during World War II exploded on 18th February 1943. The site of the old Malthouse and its cottages has now been rebuilt, but two people were killed and seven houses were destroyed. Local people recall the feathers caught in the trees from the feather beds that were blown up. In the 'Great Storm' on the night of 27th October 1987 the trees themselves were blown down. New trees were planted and now the grassy plot is the front garden of Chantry Green House. Its peaceful appearance belies its violent past history.[20]

Fig 10. The site of the old malthouse and its cottages where the German bomb exploded in 1943. Steyning Museum is beyond the red car, on the right.

---

[20] The author was very unexpectedly bitten in the leg by a dog one dark evening in November 2004, when walking past the Green thinking dark historical thoughts.

Fig. 11. Railway Approach, now Station Road, with the Booking Hall in the background, the Railway Hotel and Southdown Terrace on the right, c.1910.

Not far from Steyning Station, the Chantry Green area became a magnet for the literary and artistic set in the late-19th and early-20th century. Visitors could come down from London without too much trouble, and either side of the little green were two elegant houses whose occupants welcomed them. Chantry Green House tended to host the artistic set. Mark William Fisher R.A., the American artist, lived there, also Arthur Grace, with visitors such as James Aumonier, another Steyning resident for a while. Bertram Nicholls (1883-1974), who became President of the Royal Society of British Artists in 1931, lived in Goring Road and had a studio behind his house. His watercolour of *'Chantry Green, Steyning'* was exhibited in the 1934 Liverpool Autumn Exhibition.[21]

---

[21] F. Rutter, *Bertram Nicholls,* (1935); information from the Fine Art Department, National Museums, Liverpool, 22 March 2005.

Fig. 12. Chantry House, Steyning.

In 1935 Nicholls was commissioned to do a painting for the new trans-Atlantic liner, H.M.S. Queen Mary. It measured 9' x 7' 6" (2.74m. x 2.32m.) and was painted in the studio of Chantry House (on the west side of Chantry Green), as space was at a premium. It shows Arundel and its Roman Catholic 'Cathedral' on the South Downs, with water meadows and cattle below. The painting was hung in the rest room of the First Class Promenade Deck on the Queen Mary. Nicholls's paintings of Steyning and elsewhere can be seen in galleries in Brighton, Worthing, Manchester, Preston, Dublin, New York and Montreal. A painting of Steyning church executed in 1921 was presented to the Tate Gallery. Nicholls was a founder member of the Steyning Preservation Society (together with John Scragg, Head Master of Steyning Grammar School) in the 1930s. By the early 1960s they were the only surviving members, but on 23rd April 1963 the Steyning Society was inaugurated, a worthy successor. No scandal perhaps, but an interesting diversion.

Chantry House holds some surprising tales. In 1934 sisters Edith and Nora Shackleton Heald bought the house. Edith was a special correspondent on the Evening Standard, and the first woman to report from the House of Lords. Poet and writer W.B.Yeats described her as '...once the best paid woman journalist in the world'.[22] Norah was editor of *The Lady* from 1930 to 1953. Friends of theirs, such as Alison Settle, fashion editor, Rolfe Scott-James, writer and editor of the *London Mercury,* and Stella Gibbons, author of *Cold Comfort Farm,* were some of the many who came to stay. Stella became secretary to the editor of the *Evening Standard* in 1926 until she was sacked in 1930, when she became an editorial assistant on *The Lady.*[23] A frequent visitor was the Irish poet William Butler Yeats, who wrote some of his later poems and plays at the house. Edith possibly became his mistress in 1937. She was an ardent feminist, and at fifty-three the oldest of his late loves. There is a photograph of of Edith sunbathing topless in the garden of Chantry House while Yeats gazes admiringly at her. The excellent biography of Yeats by Brenda Maddox, *George's Ghosts,* reveals much about his relationship with Edith and their friends.[24]

Yeats died in 1939 and an extreme change came about at Chantry House. In 1942 lesbian artist Hannah Gluckstein, known as Gluck (to rhyme with 'luck' or whatever word the reader might choose) met Edith and Nora. They journeyed specially to Gluck's rented house at

---

[22] B. Maddox, *George's Ghosts: A New Life of W.B.Yeats,* (1999), 347
[23] R. Oliver, *Out of the Woodshed. The Life of Stella Gibbons,* (1998), 61, 77, 82
[24] Maddox, see Chapters Fifteen and Sixteen, and photograph between 284-285.

Plumpton, not far from Lewes in Sussex, to see a painting she had done, a small landscape of Blackdown, the highest point in Sussex. Edith and Gluck may possibly have met six years previously at the 70th birthday party of H. G. Wells at the Savoy. They spent three hours with Gluck, and this was the beginning of their friendship.

Gluck made several trips to Steyning to see Bertram Nicholls, in his capacity of Chairman of the Sussex Council of Churches. She visited the Heald sisters on these occasions and in 1944 held an exhibition of her paintings at Steyning Grammar School in Church Street. She took to spending days and nights at Chantry House and in October of the same year she moved in, taking the Yeats' room as her study. She and Edith became lovers and it led to a sad and difficult time for Nora.[25]

Gluck, born in 1895, had bravely 'come out' as a lesbian in her teens, leaving her family (though they continued to support her financially for the rest of her life), shingling her hair and wearing a man's suit. She also wore a Homburg hat and smoked a pipe. There were many 'scenes' at Chantry House, particularly in 1946. At that time Gluck was 51, Edith ten years her senior at 61, and Norah 63. Gluck caused an irrevocable split between the two sisters.

The Trust that handled Gluck's money paid half the value of Chantry House to Nora and on Valentine's Day, 1948, aged sixty-five, Nora left, moving to another house in Steyning. Diana Souhami's fascinating and well-researched biography of Gluck reveals far more than it is possible to write here, and also shows what a talented artist she was.

---

[25] D. Souhami, *Gluck 1895-1978: Her Biography,* (2001 edn); the following paragraph also draws on this.

When walking past Chantry Green and down the narrow lane on a dark winter's night, the past presses in at this point in Steyning, with Yeats, the Heald sisters, Gluck, the bomb and poor John Launder burnt at the stake.

Just round the corner to the south is Vine Cottage, at 24 Church Street. Here during the 1920s lived poet and publisher Victor Neuburg, known to his friends as 'Vickybird', who set up the Vine Press, mainly to publish his own poetry.[26]

Aleister Crowley, notorious as "The Beast" and a Black Magician, described Neuburg as '...small, dishevelled and gnome-like'. He had a slight curvature of the spine. They were both Cambridge men and in 1908 went on a walking holiday in Spain, and in 1909 to Algeria, where Crowley apparently turned Neuburg into a camel. Don't ask – read some of Crowley's biographies to find out more.[27]

Apparently Neuburg had a shambling gait, made erratic gestures, had a hangdog look and a lunatic laugh. Crowley at one point shaved his friend's head, leaving two tufts at the temples which he twisted up into horns, calling him his demon or familiar spirit – though more probably he thought of him as Pan, the god of lust and magic.

Vickybird's association with Crowley came to an end in 1914, when the former had a nervous breakdown.[28]

---

[26] After Neuburg left Steyning, he 'discovered' the young Dylan Thomas and Laurie Lee while working for a London journal.

[27] See L. Sutin, *Do What Thou Wilt: A Life of Aleister Crowley,* (2002) to begin with.

[28] See V. E. Neuburg, *Vickybird: A Memoir by his son,* (1983); A. Calder-Marshall, *The Magic of My Youth,* (1951); J. Overton Fuller, *The Magical Dilemma of Victor Neuburg: Aleister Crowley's Magical Brother & Lover,* (2nd rev. edn, 2005)

Fig. 13. Vine Cottage, 24 Church Street, on the left of the photograph.

Arthur Calder-Marshall, whose grandfather lived in Steyning in the 1920s, writes that Vine Cottage had a 'lurid reputation'. Neuburg, known to Steyning residents as 'The Mad Poet', hosted a stream of visitors at Vine Cottage. His son lists Paul Robeson, Tallulah Bankhead and Gertrude Stein amongst others. Arthur's grandfather was a consulting engineer but also a poet, and had a soft spot for Vickybird.

The young Arthur was a frequent visitor to Vine Cottage on his visits to Steyning and remembered his eccentric friend with affection. Vickybird hated litter, he shaved every third day, he wore a Norfolk jacket and knickerbockers, with holes at his elbows and knees, and frayed ends to the sleeves. The gentry of Steyning agreed that he would whisper to a child (to whom he had given a halfpenny, calling it a golden guinea), 'Now remember, there is no God!' and the vicar's wife maintained that he added, 'And tell your Daddy to vote Labour at the next election.'

In 1921 he had married Kathleen Goddard, perhaps a rather long-suffering lady. However, her lover occasionally called to take her away, with Vickybird's blessing.

Vickybird revealed to Arthur that Aleister Crowley, "The Beast", had ruined his life. Certainly Crowley made several visits to Steyning, endeavouring to worm his way back into Vickbird's affections, but without success. He banged on the door of Vine Cottage one day with his stick, and said to Kathleen 'I want Victor'. Luckily Victor was out and Kathleen closed the door in his face.

On another occasion Crowley sent his 'Scarlet Woman' (he usually had one) in his stead. She did not speak when Victor opened the door, merely opened her coat and revealed 'the Mark of the Beast' between her naked breasts. One just hopes that Mrs. Congreve-Pridgeon, the vicar's wife, was not passing at the time.

Vickybird left Steyning in the early 1930s and moved to London. He was responsible for recognising and publishing the genius of Dylan Thomas in 1933. He encouraged many other young poets too, Laurie Lee and Pamela Hansford Johnson amongst them. He died in 1940, having added a new word to the Oxford English Dictionary – 'ostrobogulous', meaning anything interesting, bizarre, unusual or bawdy. He must have applied it to much in his own life, more than a decade of it spent in Steyning.

Fig. 14. Part of the 15th century buildings of Steyning Grammar School (founded 1614), on the left of the photograph.

Moving away from all these riotous scenes, walk in a south-westerly direction, passing Steyning Grammar School on your left. At the end of Church Street, cross the High Street with care, with the mini-roundabout on your right, and turn left down the attractively paved stone causeway where a low flint wall shields you from the traffic. Just after the bow-fronted window of a former lawyer's office, you will pass a fine Queen Anne fronted building with steps leading to a porch. This is Penfold House at 17 High Street, where Charles Marshall Esquire (1761-1845) lived. He was the Duke of Norfolk's Steyning attorney and practised law from 1789 to 1840. The Duke owned many houses in the town and Marshall took care of any legal problems and also dealt with voting matters at election times. Steyning was one of the 'Rotten Boroughs', returning two Members of Parliament on 120 or so votes – only inhabitants who lived in houses 'built on old foundations' were able to vote, so corruption was rife, as can be imagined.[29] Marshall saw to it that his employer's interests were safeguarded, whatever it took, at least until the 1832 Reform Act.

Fig. 15. Penfold House, the former home of lawyer Charles Marshall.

---

[29] See W. A. Barron, 'Sidelights on Election Methods in the Eighteenth Century', **Sussex County Magazine, 24, no. 3,** (March 1950), 77-80.

A memoir of 1889 harks back to Charles Marshall and his times. 'Aunt Lizzie' Gorringe of Kingston Buci manor house (now Shoreham College), with her eccentric spelling, wrote that Marshall:-

> ...came from Kent and began life with only a sixpence in his pocket but a more corteous old Gentleman never lived. His very appearance was remarkable, as I recollect him always in black, with black silk stockings, buckled shoes, large cravet and frilled shirt. Mrs. Marshall always wore a Turban and false hair, little curls round her face, white in the daytime and coloured for dress. Mrs. Marshall was renowned for her gay dressing, she was a very handsome woman noted for her kindness, hospitality and many charities...This Mr. and Mrs. Marshall lived at Steyning in the old house with lime trees in front where the Miss Penfolds now live, and the old lawyers offices still remain as they were in Mr. Marshall's time.

Fig. 16. The Causeway, High Street, Steyning,
with the bow-fronted window of the former lawyer's offices.

They had two daughters, very attractive girls, and as they were known to be wealthy they were made much of, and their mother Mrs. Marshall was very careful to keep them away from the Military in the town. The army in those days was not as it is now, and an Officer was not considered a good match for a young lady of wealth and position. Regiments were very badly Officered in those days, poor Irish Adventurers of dissapated habits...

...the eldest [Miss Marshall], Sarah, married Mr. Penfold of Rustington and the younger, Mary, married the Rev. Griffith, at that time curate in charge of Sompting. These young ladies were believed to have £50,000 when they married and more after that...[30]

This memoir, mentioning the Barracks, reminds us that Steyning was a garrison town, with a regiment always quartered there. They were built c.1804 because of the Napoleonic Wars.

Though demolished by 1819, the field where they stood, called Barrack Field for most of the nineteenth century, comprised much of what is now covered in housing, between Jarvis Lane and Goring Road. Military buttons and remnants of epaulettes have been found in the gardens.[31]

---

[30] W. A. Heasman & J. Pennington, 'Aunt Lizzie's Story – a description of Annington, Kingston Buci and Steyning in the Nineteenth Century', **West Sussex History, 73,** (Spring. 2004), 32-37
[31] Information from Joyce Sleight of Steyning

Fig. 17. The east end of Steyning High Street c.1920, called Singwell Street before the mid-nineteenth century. Springwells Hotel is on the left hand side.

Walk past Springwells Hotel and pause before turning up Dog Lane.

Take yourself back to 1634, mount your horse and ride towards Lancing to discover what happened to John Blackman about 7pm on 20th September in that year. He was probably riding down Maudlin Lane, heading for the Annington, Botolphs and Coombes roads, and so on to Lancing, though there would have been various bridle routes he could have taken to shorten this.

However, Blackman did not get to his Lancing home, wherever that was. He no doubt passed Dog Lane on the way to an accident waiting to happen.

Fig. 18. The Dog Lane nameplate. Half a century ago a 'No Parking' notice was erected here, whereupon a local wag (sorry…) changed the P to a B, so that it read 'Dog Lane. No Barking beyond this Corner'. *E. W. Cox & F. Duke, In and Around Steyning,* (1954), 44-45

The Coroner's Inquest of 22nd September 1634 (probably held at the White Horse Inn)[32] reveals what happened. Seventeen local jurors,

---

[32] All references to Steyning inns are to be found in J. Pennington, 'The Inns and Taverns of Western Sussex, 1550-1700: A Regional Study of Their Architectural and Social History', (unpublished doctoral thesis, University of Southampton, 2003). Copies available at Steyning Museum, the West Sussex Record Office, Chichester, Worthing Library Local History Studies Centre, Sussex Archaeological Society's Library, Lewes, and University Libraries of Chichester and Southampton, or through Inter-Library Loan.

including an innkeeper, heard that Blackman had mounted his horse at Steyning about 7pm two days previously, and had ridden towards Lancing. About 8pm he was found lying on the ground before he had ridden 'two furlonges' (about a quarter of a mile) from Steyning. Presumably whoever had seen him lying there thought that he would recover eventually and continue on his way. Blackman lay on the ground until 3am on 21st September, when he was carried from the road to a nearby house, dying within the hour.

The jurors decided that he fell from the horse, 'which fall and his lying on the ground for 6 or 7 hours and wine were the causes of his death.' He had obviously been overdoing his drinking in Steyning. His widow, Margaret, was taking care of the horse, valued at £1 6s. 8d. [c.£110] in case it may have been '…forfeit to the King, or to Thomas, earl of Arundel and Surrey, Earl Marshall, lord of the liberty.'[33]

Blackman may have been drinking at the White Horse, which would have supplied wine. Two inns held wine licences at that time, and the other may have been the Chequer. There were several more inns around the market area of the High Street, the Crown and the Blue Anchor lay between the White Horse and the Chequer, while across the road the Swan (which by 1646 had changed its name to the George), sited at what is now 46-52 High Street to the west of the Post Office, and the Spread Eagle (which later became the Kings Arms) at the corner of Bank Passage, though this has been rebuilt.

A large market-house stood in the middle of the street here, impeding the traffic (see below).

---

[33] R. F. Hunnisett, *Sussex Coroners' Inquests 1603-1688,* (Public Record Office, 1998), 83-84

There were several alehouses too, though their whereabouts is difficult to determine as they often did not last very long. Etheldred Taylor of Steyning ran one in 1646, possibly near Springwells Hotel in the east end of the High Street, then called Singwell Street (Sing not Spring, the water can still be heard singing under the road on a quiet night), and he was fined 2s. 6d. for being unlicensed (12½p. now, but the equivalent of c.£9 then) at the Petworth Easter Quarter Sessions in April of that year. John Washer of Steyning was also fined for the same reason at another unnamed alehouse.

Taylor was soon licensed 'to keep a common alehouse' in the town. He was a tailor by name as well as by occupation, and also an alehousekeeper – his wife probably worked with him. He was bound by sureties of £10, guaranteed by his brewer Thomas Longmer, and John Michell, a local carpenter, in the sums of £5 each. This money would have been forfeit if Taylor's alehouse was not well governed. The Justices of the Peace kept an eye on the alehouses, usually a good source of money from the fines they applied.

Whether John Gillam of Steyning, a currier (leather worker),[34] drank in either of these alehouses is unknown, but he was fined 10s. in the same court as Taylor and Washer, for shooting pigeons with a handgun.[35]

Pigeons were a valuable source of meat, eggs and saltpetre. Their dovecotes were an important part of the local economy.

---

[34] Curriers converted the hard, uneven leathers produced by the tanner into a uniform, attractive material, ready to go on to the shoemaker; it was a long, hard job.
[35] B. C. Redwood, 'Quarter Sessions Order Book, 1642-1649', **SRS, 54,** (1954), 94-95

However, Gillam's ghost might be welcomed in the High Street today by some of the inhabitants of the town (see Fig. 28).

Fig. 19. Dog Lane, heading south-west. The dog-leg bend is at the top on the right.

Turn by Springwells Hotel and walk up Dog Lane, where the stream may be running if the weather has been wet. Take the first dog leg (just a bend and nothing to do with the name) to the right. Dogs were once kennelled in Dog Lane and used for various activities.

The dogs, some possibly used for hare coursing, and some for the postcarts, also had another function. Their 'droppings' were a vital part of the leather industry, used in the tanning process to soften the leather.

Those interested in this very smelly process can read more about it at Steyning Museum.[36]

In the 19th century Steyning's tanyard moved from this end of the town, where it was sited in the Wickham Close area (across the High Street from Dog Lane), to the other. Two breweries were using the Dog Lane water source, which presumably caused problems to the tanning processes. The stream that runs by the Star Inn at the north-west end of the High Street was then utilised for the town's leather industry until the tanyard closed in 1941.

Back in Dog Lane, the use of dogs for the post carts was stopped in the mid-19th century, though from illustrations they seemed to have enjoyed it, particularly when a rabbit or hare came into sight.

Sadly, in 1813, Miss Steer, the Steyning postmaster's daughter, was committed to gaol for stealing the letters that her father was supposed to deliver.[37]

---

[36] J. Pennington, 'Noysome savours and evell Ayers', **Steyning Museum Newsletter,** (December 2000), 2-3.
[37] J. Greenwood, *The Posts of Sussex: The Chichester Branch 1250-1840,* (1973), 75

Dog Lane emerges opposite the former stables of the White Horse Inn. The main inn burned down in 1949 (on the night of Steyning Fire Brigade's annual dance elsewhere in the town), and was rehoused in the stables and coach house at the rear. Just one old part remains (see Fig. 39), the range with the Horsham stone roof, dating from c.1500.

Fig. 20. The former stables of the White Horse Inn, seen from Dog Lane; the main buildings burnt down in 1949.

Thomas Turner was a grocer in East Hoathly, a small village between Heathfield and Lewes in the east of Sussex. He lodged at the old White Horse in 1761 when he visited a friend in Steyning.

Turner kept a diary, and the interesting and amusing entries for 1754-1765 have been published. He had earlier visited Thomas Burfield of

Steyning, who supplied him with beehives. This trip may just have been an excuse for a 'boys' night out', as apparently Burfield was 'a man very much given to drink'.[38]

Turner set out from East Hoathly with a friend, Thomas Durrant, on 8th November, 1756, leaving at 11.30 a.m. They called at Falmer and Patcham, apparently to feed the horses, but as the Swan and the Black Lion were (and are still) at those two villages, they no doubt took on their own liquid refreshment.

They did not arrive at Steyning until the evening, when Turner became 'not very sober' with his friend Burfield, who took them about the town drinking. He had to leave his riding companion behind when he went home the next day, as Thomas '...actually was past riding, or almost anything else...'. Dame Durrant (Thomas's mother) '...was like to tear me to pieces with words for leaving her son behind'. It had obviously been a good outing.[39]

On Turner's visit in 1761, he says that he lodged at the White Horse but dined at the Chequer. He obviously preferred the food at the latter inn where he ate cold duck pasty and two roasted rabbits. Another meal at the Chequer comprised a boiled leg of mutton with turnips and cabbage. He does not relate what he had to drink on this occasion; perhaps remembering his previous visit he was a little more abstemious.

He reports, rather smugly, 'I came home very safe and sober'.[40]

---

[38] D. Vaisey, (ed.), *The Diary of Thomas Turner 1754-1765,* (1994 edn), 2, 72, 202, 217
[39] Ibid., 71-72
[40] Ibid., 234-235

Turn left at the top of Dog Lane, then take the first right into White Horse Square and continue along Charlton Street when you will soon see the Police Station on your left, built c.1860. A fine Victorian building, it is well worth architectural study, with its randomly placed field flints and smart brickwork.

Fig. 21. The Police Station, Steyning, built c.1860.

Before this was built, any miscreants had been held at the old market-house gaol, first of all on the ground floor of a building (demolished in 1771) which stood in the middle of the High Street between nos. 33-35 on the south-east side, and 46-52 on the north-west side (see Fig. 37 below). The old market-house would have looked something like the Titchfield market hall from Hampshire, now re-erected at the Weald and Downland Open Air Museum at Singleton, near Chichester (see Fig. 36).

The 'new' market-house (now called the 'Old Market House') was built at 72 High Street, with recycled materials from the old one, where it can be seen today, with its fine clock on top of the roof.

Fig. 22. The Old Market House, 72 High Street, Steyning, an example of 18th century recycling.

Both market-houses had a small lock-up. In 1815 there were "Girls in the Cage" (cage often being the description for the barred cell in a market-house) which caused a problem to the parish officers when some men needed a temporary prison for two days. They could not be locked up with the 'Girls' in the same space, so had the misfortune (presumably) to be housed in the Chequer Inn instead, hopefully not in the cellars. The men would probably have been awaiting removal to the County Gaol at Horsham. The old gaol there was demolished thirty years later, in 1845, and Steyning-born Henry Michell, a successful brewer and businessman, put in a tender to demolish the building. He was successful, bidding £2,560 and making a profit of £5,000. He recycled two and a half million bricks, some of which can be seen in Steyning today. They are quite distinctive and anyone interested can see some on the remaining tanyard building in Tanyard Lane (see map), the tallest on the north side of the road, the former warehouse.

Fig. 23. The tall building is the former warehouse of Steyning's tanyard – the bricks came from Horsham gaol, another example of 18th century recycling. The new houses on the left hand side are built on part of the old tanyard.

Michell opened the gaol to public view, when thousands of people came to see the "Condemned cell" and the "murderer's grave". The rubble was recycled, producing a mile of ballast for the Horsham to London Railway. The 15,000 square feet of Horsham paving slabs, 100 iron doors, 150 iron windows were all sold for re-use. Many of the bricks were used for the railway bridge over the river Ouse at Lewes, and bridges on the railway between Three Bridges and Horsham.[41]

Steyning's old market-house and Horsham's old gaol - not particularly scandalous, but revealing two episodes of eighteenth century recycling.

Fig. 24. The blue lamp at Steyning Police Station.

[41] K. Neale, *Victorian Horsham: The Diary of Henry Michell 1809-1874,* (1975), 43-47

Continue along Charlton Street, leaving the Police Station on your left and shortly turn into the Chequer Yard on the right. You can imagine this as a busy inn yard in the sixteenth and seventeenth centuries.

Fig. 25. The Chequer Inn yard, with the ostler's house in the centre. The High Street can be seen through the arch on the right. The rear of the inn and the former stables are on the left of the photograph.

In 1579 James Holland, innkeeper and churchwarden, was reported by one of the sidesmen at St. Andrew's Church. Holland may have been the landlord of the Chequer Inn, as widow Joan Holland was paying rent for the inn to the Wiston Estate in 1622. The sneaky sidesman had been prowling about the town the Sunday before St. James' Day (25th July) in the 22nd year of the reign of Queen Elizabeth I and wrote '...I

43

went out of the church to see good rule according to myne othes [oaths], and I came and found James Holand, inkeper, one of the church wardens, and Richard Pellet and John Kok drynkyng in the servistime'.[42] Holland's duties as churchwarden probably continued but he may have been fined.

Fig. 26. The Chequer Inn, High Street, Steyning, early 20th century.

The Chequer was the scene of many River Dinners in earlier centuries. Landowners who had to cope with the river Adur in flood, the unblocking of sluices and the clearance of streams and ditches had formed a local group, known as the Sewer Commissioners in the eighteenth century. They met to discuss problems, applied a local tax to help with any works needed, and had an annual dinner at a local inn. The Chequer in Steyning was a favourite venue, and a menu survives for 'The River Dinner March 3rd 1899' at the inn. Ten members gathered for their meal at 2pm.

---

[42] WSRO, EP1/23/5

The amounts eaten were certainly rather scandalous...read on and remember the time and the number of diners:-

*First course* - *about 4lbs of salmon with cucumbers, potatoes and lobster sauce*

*Second course* - *roast beef, leg of mutton, two fowls and a tongue. Accompanying vegetables – cauliflower, baked and boiled potatoes, secale, melted butter, caper sauce and bread sauce*

*Third course* – *two plum puddings, two custards, three jellies, one blancmange, two jam tarts*

*Fourth course* – *Bread and cheese, celery and butter*

*Dessert* – *Oranges, apples, two sorts of nuts as well as almonds, raisins, and mixed biscuits*

*Tea and coffee and bread and butter and cake at 4 o'clock. Edie and Annie were the cooks, Mr. Searle was the waiter*

One can imagine the waistcoats straining across bulging stomachs. There is nothing to indicate how much they had to drink…

Mrs. Edith Chalcraft's late-nineteenth century account books contain much of interest – she was the great-grandmother of the late Colin Garlick, who was landlord of the Chequer Inn from 1948-1990.[43] Presumably the eleven pounds of suet she used for 20 home-made plum puddings for another large feast at the inn came from one of the local butchers.

---

[43] J. Pennington, *The Chequer Inn, Steyning: Five centuries of innkeeping in a Sussex market town,* (1990), 34-39

Fig. 27. The author with the late Colin and Norma Garlick of the Chequer Inn, 39 High Street, Steyning (photograph taken in 1990).

The account books show that Mrs. Chalcraft tactfully shared her meat order between the three High Street butchers, Cherryman, King and Street, as to favour just one would have presumably caused difficulties or local jealousies. There is a butcher's bill tucked into the back of one book noting ox tongue and salt beef of over 10lbs each, which she boiled for two hours.

A supper for 24 bell ringers in 1881consisted of 13lbs of boiled beef, a leg of mutton, 14lbs of pork loin, two plum puddings and four of tapioca. The choir ate, or were offered, 29lbs of beef, a ham, a tongue, a turkey and three fowls, as well as bread and apples.

Fig. 28. Chanctonbury Butchers, 51 High Street, Steyning, on the right hand side of the photograph. It has been a butcher's shop since at least 1670. Note the pigeons clustering around the imitation bird of prey on the roof.

The butchers were an important part of the local economy and at least two shops were functioning in the seventeenth century, one at what is now Chanctonbury Butchers, 51 High Street, certainly a butcher's shop since 1670 and probably earlier, and the other at 42 High Street (see Fig. 29), selling meat in 1730 and also probably much earlier. Butchers tended to stay in the same place as the shop design would have been pertinent to the trade, and there was usually a slaughterhouse at the back, as butchers killed their own animals until well into the twentieth century.

If only we had some of those early prices. What about sixteenth century London with 'Pieces of beef weighing two pounds and a half at the least, yea, three pounds or better, for a penny on every butcher's stall in the City.'[44] Joints of meat were much bigger than they are now, and were originally sold by appearance, rather than by weight. Weighing grew slowly in popularity in the seventeenth century and caused many problems. Scales were costly and butchers started to leave more blood in the carcasses to make the meat heavier. They also pinned in pieces of fat, as fat was seen as very desirable, adding to the flavour of the meat.

Steyning must have smelt very different in the past, with the tanyard, breweries and slaughterhouses. Butcher's Hall Lane in London was known as 'Stinking Lane' originally, and was in the middle of the Shambles. It was rechristened just before Shakespeareans had a chance to point out that the road by any other name would smell of meat. Come on, you can work it out...[45]

Philip Gosse, who wrote several books about Sussex, reminisced about pre-World War II holidays at Dunster in Somerset as a boy, where one of his particular friends was the son of the village butcher:-

> I remember very well my pride when one day the butcher allowed me to kill a bullock all by myself. The poor terrified brute had a rope put round its neck, which

---

[44] D. Davis, *A History of Shopping,* (1966), 86
[45] Ibid. 84; a play on William Shakespeare's words - 'A rose by any other name would smell as sweet', from *Romeo and Juliet,* (1594).

was passed through a hole in a block of wood. When the rope was in place my friends tugged on it until the head of the beast rested on the block. Then I seized the executioner's pole-axe by its long wooden handle and with one unerring blow brought the point of the pole-axe on the middle of the bullock's forehead, driving the iron point through its skull into its brain. The beast quivered for a moment and then fell dead in a relaxed heap. We boys looked upon those summer days spent at the slaughter-house as well spent and suffered no qualms whatever.[46]

Inventories of goods and chattels that survive for some of Steyning's butchers in the seventeenth century show that they had comfortable homes and well-stocked shops, with slaughterhouses containing pole-axes, ropes and other tackle. There was usually a well nearby.

The butchers wore 'shop clothes', probably aprons, had elm blocks and several types of cleavers and butcher's hooks, as well as specialised weighing scales called 'stilliards' or steel yards.[47]

A sad incident happened in a Steyning slaughter house in 1587, when James Easton hanged himself with a rope attached to a beam there. A verdict of suicide was recorded and possibly some of the jurors knew the circumstances of his imbalance of mind.[48] The Coroners' Inquests open a window on such tragic occurrences.

---

[46] P. Gosse, *Go To The Country,* (1935), 83-84
[47] See the Pennington/Sleight collection of inventories, wills and probate accounts at Steyning Museum.
[48] Hunnisett, (1996), 89

*The Sussex Weekly Advertiser,* 25th April 1803, gives a lively account of an incident involving Mr. Gates' butchers shop at 42 High Street, when:-

On Monday last a bull, belonging to Mr. Gates, butcher, ran wildly through the town of Steyning, attempting to toss every person that stood in his way, but only succeeded in throwing one, an athletic sack-weaver, who whilst he was down, actually took the bull by the horns, and held him, till he was relieved by others from his perilous situation.

Fig. 29. Wood's Butchers, 42 High Street, Steyning, 2006. The shop ceased trading in 1988. It had been a butcher's shop since at least the early-18th century.

The athletic sack-weaver, whoever he was, must have been the hero of the hour, if not the week, and it is to be hoped that Mr. Gates rewarded him with a good joint of beef.

So, let us go from meat to murder four centuries ago. You may need to sit down in one of Steyning's pubs, restaurants or teashops to digest the next few pages.

In 1593 the Coroner's Court met in Steyning, almost certainly at the White Horse, on 24th February. On 9th January, John Cook, a Steyning yeoman, had murdered Peter Cook in the town:-

> ...striking him on the head with a staff worth 4d. which he held in both hands and giving him several fatal wounds and then immediately taking his head in his hands and breaking his neck, of which wounds and breaking he immediately died. No one else was privy to the death to the jurors' knowledge.

This was a complicated case and presumably the Cooks were related, perhaps brothers or cousins. Alice Cook was meant to attend the Assize Court just two days' later, on 26th February, but defaulted. It was pleaded on her behalf '...that she was in such an advanced stage of pregnancy that she could not attend without great peril to her life'.

In June Alice Cook was described as a widow, and it is clear that Peter Cook, the dead man, had been her husband, and that she was suspected of involvement in the murder. Cecily Cook, the wife of John Cook the suspected murderer, and two local labourers were to give evidence against Alice. Reading between the lines, it could be wondered whether Alice was pregnant by John Cook. However, that will never be known, and at the Assizes of 16th July '...Alice appeared and was discharged because nothing was found against her'. Nothing was said about her pregnancy and what happened to John Cook is not recorded.[49]

A couple of years later a Coroner's Court was in session at Bramber, on 9th September 1595. The White Lion Inn there (now rebuilt on the same site and called the Castle Hotel) had a Court Room on the first floor where the 14 jurors, all local men who would have known the people involved, were sitting.

Four days before, on 5th September, William Price of Henfield, a shoemaker (remember James a Barowe, a troublesome shoemaker of Henfield in 1547, above) '...feloniously killed John Nitingall at Steyning...giving him a wound on the left side of the head of which he languished at Bramber until 7th September and then died'. After the murder Price fled from Steyning '...but whither the jurors do not know'. He may have got away with it, because at the time of the Assizes he was still at large.[50]

Half a century on, a very sad case appears in the records. The Coroner's Court sat again in Steyning, on 17th March 1648 (the year before the execution of Charles I). Thirteen jurors heard how William Dunstall of Steyning, aged 11, had been beaten to death by Thomas Juppe on 6th March.

Juppe was described as 'late of Steyning' and a yeoman. He had used a 'hasell driveing goad' which he held in both hands, 'violently striking and beating the boy on the back and hips at Ashurst'. He languished (there is much languishing described in the Coroners' records) until

---

[49] Hunnisett, (1996), 111-112
[50] Ibid., 119. WSRO, PAR 183/2/20 where the Steyning Parish Register merely states that 'Nitingale' was buried. There is no mention of his murder.

11pm on the same day, and then died. At the Assize court Juppe was charged with murder, together with Richard White, another yeoman, late of Steyning. Juppe had actually done the beating while White aided and abetted him.

The Grand Jury rejected the charge against White and reduced that against Juppe to manslaughter. Juppe pleaded not guilty but was convicted. He successfully pleaded benefit of clergy (see below) and was bailed to appear at the next Assize Court. In the meantime he was to procure a pardon for branding on the hand. Whether this took place is uncertain.[51]

Benefit of clergy was originally the privilege granted to the clergy of being handed over from a civil to an ecclesiastical court for trial for a capital offence. This was extended in England to all who could read, and so who could, theoretically, become clerics.

Prisoners read a verse from a Latin Bible, later an English one. First offenders read the first verse of Psalm 51 'Misere mei, Deus...'. After the Reformation the English version could be read 'Have mercy upon me, O God...' and was known as the 'Neck Verse'. It became a useful legal fiction to mitigate the severity of the law for first offenders and was used by the courts to avoid a capital sentence.

The base of a guilty person's thumb might be branded with a T (for Tyburn) to prevent anyone claiming again, and this is presumably what was to happen to Juppe of Steyning. The test of reading a Biblical verse was abolished in 1706 and the whole procedure stopped in 1827.[52]

---

[51] Ibid. (1998), 100
[52] D. Hey, (ed.), *The Oxford Companion to Local and Family History,* (1999 reprint), 38-39

In 1588, the year of the Spanish Armada, a benefit of clergy pleading had taken place in Steyning. Some familiar surnames appear in the list of jurors, Peter and John Cook, and a Thomas Dunstall.

On 14th June Thomas Dape, a local mason, murdered Thomas Gregory with a dagger, stabbing him on the right side of his chest, and he died immediately. A local doctor would have been called to examine the body and make a report - the wound was one inch long and five inches deep. Dape had been sent to gaol by the Coroner, but pleaded not guilty and was acquitted of murder but convicted of manslaughter. He successfully pleaded benefit of clergy.[53]

Another Gregory family member was murdered some years later, on 13th December in 1624. This time it was Richard Gregory, murdered by James Crowdson, a Steyning labourer, who stabbed him in the abdomen with a little knife, causing Gregory's immediate death. Crowdson pleaded not guilty of manslaughter, pleaded benefit of clergy, failed to read, and was hanged. His guilt was presumably well known, though he had been acquitted of murder.[54] One wonders just how safe it was to walk down the High Street in those days.

Stabbings in the High Street were nothing new. Sixty years earlier a fight had ended with a murder. Thomas Osborne of Wickham (a farm settlement to the north of Steyning but in the parish), labourer, was in the market place[55] at Steyning, when John Miles came and struck him

---

[53] Hunnisett, (1996), 92-93; WSRO, PAR 183/2/20, the Parish Register entry states 'Thomas Gregorie murdered by Thomas Dapp 14th June, buried 16th June'.
[54] Ibid., (1998), 66; WSRO, PAR 183/2/20, the Parish Register entry states 'Rychard Gregory: a young man – slayne – buryed 13 December 1624'.
[55] The market place was based around the old market-house, in the middle of the street. It stretched from the Chequer Inn to the White Horse, and would have overflowed around the cross-roads into Church Street and what is now Sheep Pen Lane.

with a dagger which he held in his left hand. Osborne's life was despaired of, but he managed to flee from Miles as far as he could.

However, Miles pursued him '...to the wall of John Guilham's dwelling-house beyond which Osborne could not escape without imminent danger to his life'. In desperation, Osborne killed Miles in self defence with his own dagger, noted as having been held in his right hand. The wound, made with the dagger's point, was half an inch wide and two inches deep, under the left side of Miles's abdomen. Miles languished until the next day and then died.[56]

Osborne went to gaol, was later pardoned, and sadly died a natural death while in prison in Southwark on 19th March 1566, about six weeks after the fight.[57]

Walk on down the High Street, avoiding sharp objects, pass the Fire Station on your left, and soon after passing the Star Inn on your right,[58] turn left into Sir George's Place and pass the row of cottages on your right as you walk up the hill.

At the top, on the right, it is possible to glimpse Court Mill, which stopped working in 1927 and was turned into a dwelling house some three years later.

Both water and windmills were often scenes of ghastly accidents, due to heavy machinery and lack of safety precautions. William Parker, a

---

[56] Ibid., (1996), 7
[57] The King's Bench prison in St. George's parish in Southwark, Surrey, was known as 'The Clink', which name became a widespread euphemism for gaol.
[58] WSRO, Wiston Ms. 5591, the Star was called the Rose and Crown in 1639.

Quaker, was 'drowned in the Upar Mill Pond' in Steyning in 1724, presumably at Court Mill.[59]

Fig. 30. Court Mill, Steyning, also known as West Mill and Charlton Court Mill in former times. It was owned by the Wiston Estate for many centuries.

In 1602 Elizabeth Pepper 'carelessly went too close to 'the swypes' of the windmill at Wappingthorn, when '...one of the sweeps struck her on the head whereby she immediately died'. John Leedes of Wappingthorn was the owner of the mill and action was taken against him. As a man of some social standing and power he managed to avoid

---

[59] P. Lucas, 'Some Notes on the Early Sussex Quaker Registers', **SAC, 55,** (1912), 87. Gatewick Mill, demolished in 1878, had its own pond too.

legal proceedings; in 1605 he was recorded as being dead and what happened then is unknown. Presumably no compensation was paid to anyone. Edward Chiles of Steyning was the miller, grinding wheat and other grain for local farmers, though he does not seem to have been in trouble for the accident.[60] Poor Elizabeth Pepper – perhaps connected with Pepper's Farm at Ashurst to the north of Wappingthorn.

Turn down the footpath to the north of Court Mill. Cross the stream (there might be a glimpse of the old mill wheel on your left if the trees are not in leaf). Turn to the right at the end, watching out for mud, and exit into Mouse Lane, the old road to Wiston House. This deeply sunken old road leads to Wiston House to the west, and is often running with water.

Fig. 31. Mouse Lane, Steyning, leading to Wiston House.

---

[60] Hunnisett, (1996), 145

Turn right, back towards Steyning High Street, and you will soon see the Old Workhouse Cottages on your left.

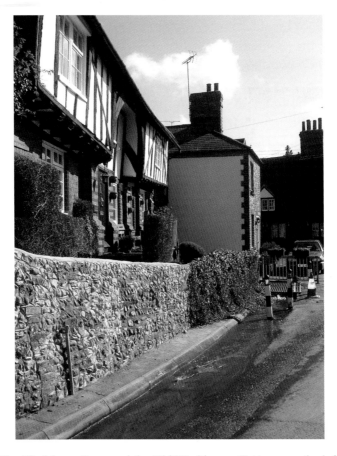

Fig. 32. Mouse Lane and the Old Workhouse Cottages on the left.

This attractive Wealden-type house (like Bayleaf at the Weald & Downland Open Air Museum at Singleton) was probably built in the mid-fifteenth century. It became the Steyning Poor House in 1775 when the parish purchased it for £100. In 1784 the Steyning Parish Registers show that a foundling from the Workhouse was baptised on 18th January. He was given the name of Moses Steyning. He was presumably found at the door of the Workhouse in watery Mouse Lane, perhaps in a basket, placed there by an unknown and grieving mother. Little Moses did not live very long, as he was buried 'a pauper' on 25th April in 1787, only three years later.[61]

Fig. 33. The Old Workhouse, Mouse Lane, Steyning.

The poor of the town had a reasonable regime at the Workhouse then - but in 1834 after the Poor Law Amendment Act all this changed. On 11th September 1835 a riot took place when the inmates were told they were to be moved to the new workhouse at Shoreham, known as the Steyning Union Workhouse. A temporary holding house at Henfield, looked after by a former Sergeant of Artillery, had been arranged. It

---

[61] WSRO, PAR 183/2/22

was feared that families were to be split up, with husbands and wives separated from their children. Unsurprisingly, they didn't want to go. A fist fight broke out, the Justices of the Peace were called, stones were thrown and hair was pulled. The Militia arrived, the Riot Act was no doubt read, and several former workhouse inhabitants ended up in Horsham gaol. A difficult and heart-breaking time for Steyning's poor.[62]

Cross the road with care, passing George Inn House (see below), heading back up the High Street and glancing left at the former Quaker Meeting House, now called Penn's House, originally Town End House.

Fig. 34. The former Quaker Meeting House, with the 20th century housing complex, Penn's Court, on the right and behind.

[62] J. Sleight, 'The Poor Law in Steyning: II. Riot and a new regime', **West Sussex History, 22,** (May 1982), 19-24

When Penn's Court, was built, the former Quaker burying ground was disturbed. The bodies were taken up and reinterred at the Brighton Meeting House ground. The females were buried on one side of the path at Steyning and males on the other, presumably so that nothing scandalous could occur after their deaths. The Quaker converts were very brave and there were quite a number locally; the first Steyning Register commences in 1651.[63] Quakers George Fox and Alexander Parker did not hold a meeting in 1655 in the Old Market House at 72 High Street, as has long been thought, but in the earlier market-house that stood right in the middle of the High Street further east. It is clearly marked on the map of 1763. The building was demolished in 1771, because of the new Turnpike Road that had been expected since 1764.

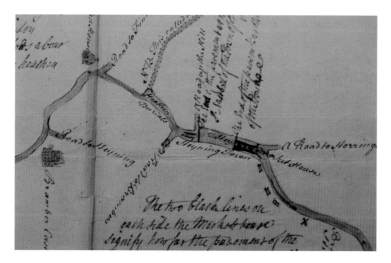

Fig. 35. Part of a sketch map of Steyning, dated 1763, showing the position of the old market-house. It is the pink square in the middle of the High Street. Note that Church Street, which should be opposite A Road up the Hill, has been omitted by the draughtsman. *West Sussex Record Office, Add. Ms. 37,522*

---

[63] Lucas, 86

61

Fig. 36. The Titchfield Market Hall, Hampshire, re-erected at the Weald & Downland Open Air Museum, Singleton, West Sussex, 1988.

The new market-house – now called the Old Market House at 72 High Street – was constructed on a vacant plot from the recycled materials from the old. You can read about this in Steyning Museum.[64]

Walk back up the High Street, note the Old Market House at 72 High Street, and then imagine the even older one in the centre of the street further east, looking something like the Titchfield Market Hall above. How it would slow up the traffic today. It was seen as an obstruction in 1771, when horse traffic would have been the problem, particularly on market day.

---

[64] J. Pennington, 'The Market-houses of Steyning', **SAC, 144,** (2006), 169-76; 'The Market Houses of Steyning', **Steyning Museum Newsletter,** (October 2005).

Fig. 37. The cyclist is walking across the approximate site of Steyning's former market-house which stood between 33-35 High Street on the left and 46-52 High Street on the right. Imagine a building like Fig. 36 there.

Fig. 38. Looking across the High Street towards the Post Office at 44. The buildings to the left are on the site of the former Swan Inn, which later became the George. The old market-house would have been in the middle of the street.

63

Stop at the former carriage entrance to the Chequer Inn yard, on your right hand side, and look across the road, past the zebra crossing, to numbers 46-52 High Street, the block of buildings to the west of the Post Office at 44. These buildings, which need further investigation, probably comprise or conceal an earlier building and its cellars, formerly the George Inn, later the Kings Head, but known as the Swan in the early-seventeenth century.

The building that stands on the corner at the north end of Steyning, opposite the entrance to Mouse Lane, known as George Inn House, only became the George Inn after 1752 when the George (above) next to the Post Office became the Kings Head.[65]

However, the following pages reveal the events that took place in the Swan Inn yard in 1610. It is an upsetting story – and was certainly a terrible and tragic scandal at the time. Imagine going under the arched entrance way between 52 and 54 High Street, (it is now private property) which leads into the back yard (often called a 'backside' in earlier times) of the former inn where there would have been stables, probably a coach house and other support buildings for an inn.

The Quarter Sessions' Rolls at the West Sussex Record Office in Chichester reveal the details of the court case, though unfortunately the foot of the document is damaged and the end of the story is unknown. However, the outcome was a foregone conclusion.

Thomas Starke (his age and home town are unknown) was in deadly trouble.[66] Various witnesses gave their depositions to the court. The

---

[65] J. Pennington, unpublished research, forthcoming.
[66] I have been unable to find the surname Starke, or any variation of it, in the Steyning Parish Registers.

following tale unfolds in the language and spelling of the time, and involves graphic sexual description. Punctuation has been inserted for ease of understanding:-

Sussex. The informaco[in] (sic) of John Baulcombe of the age of nyneteen yeares or thereabout, sworne and examined about Thom[as] Starke being accused of the Buggering of a mare,[67] take(n) before S[i]r Thom[a]s Leedes, Knight, one of his ma[jes]tes Justices, the 11th of Julye 1610.

This examinant saith that the Eleaventh of Julye 1610, being Wensday and m[ar]kett day at Stenning, in the affter noone, he requested Thom[a]s Sterke to help him catch a horse in the Backside of his father in lawes howse, dwelling at the Inne called the Swanne in Stenning, w[hi]ch he did, and the Cause why he intreated this Thom[a]s Sterke's help was by reason of the unrulynes of the said horse,[68] p[re]Fering oftentymes to horse[69] a mare that was loose in the backside.[70] But Thom[a]s Sterke, having tyed the horse by the mare, made both the horse and mare more unrulye, soe as they brake loose againe, wherupon Thom[a]s Starke tooke the mare and Carried[71] her into a Close roome. When Thom[a]s Starke was in the stable w[i]th the mare, he

---

[67] Not the mayor of Steyning, as one 20th century listener to this tale had at first imagined – the town did not have a mayor.
[68] Horse as a noun = stallion
[69] Horse as a verb = mount, mate with, service
[70] Loose in the backside = loose/free in the inn's back yard
[71] Carried her = led her

made fast the dore to him, willing this Examinant to hold the horse still in the backside. But, this examinant tying the horse to the pale[72] and com[m]ing along by the stable dore, and looking into the stable by a boord that was broken, saw Thom[a]s Sterk (as he thought) suspiciously about the mare, whereupon this examinant went to a little out howse close to the stable, and by a hole there looked in, and sawe that Thom[a]s Sterk had removed the mare to the further end of the stable, and turning her taile to the maunger,[73] he had gotten himself up into the maunger, and taking the bridle in one hand and holding th[e] other upon the saddle, he drew the mare close up to the maunger, and then drawing his yard[74] and not undoing his hose,[75] this examinant sawe him take up the taile of the mare and doe his good will (as this examinant thought) to Bugger the mare, but whether his yard went into the mare or noe this examinant cannot tell, only he can say that Thom[a]s Sterke's breeches were a little wett betweene the legges and the mare alsoe, but whither the wettnes in the mare was by reason of the horse that before offered to horse her, this examinant cannot tell.

John Bawlcome - his m(ar)ke

The penalty for this act was death by hanging and this would presumably have been known to Bawlcombe, whose father-in-law John

---

[72] Pale = fence post
[73] Maunger = manger
[74] Yard = I will leave this to your imagination, but the Oxford English Dictionary gives some helpful examples of the word's use.
[75] Hose = breeches, drawers

Cox was the landlord of the inn.[76] Events began to get out of hand as other witnesses gathered. Bawlcombe perhaps had not considered that his friend, or acquaintance, Starke, would be arrested for what was a capital offence. The Calendar of Assizes for Sussex during the reign of Elizabeth I lists five cases of what was then called buggery – sexual intercourse with an animal. Four horses and one cow were involved. Three men were sentenced to hang, one died in gaol and one outcome is unknown.[77]

The fact that John Bawlcombe was obviously spying on someone or something through a hole in the inn's stable meant that natural curiosity took over when another person passed by. William Munnery, who was about sixteen years old, gave his deposition after Bawlcombe's. The document continues:-

This examinant saith that com[m]ing along the backside of the Swanne at Stenning, seeing John Bawlcome looking in at a hole into the stable, he came to him, being beckoned unto by the said Bawlcome to come softlye, he sawe Thom[a]s Sterke standing in the maunger w[i]th his yard out, and a gray mare Close to him. And this is all that this examinant can say. Soe he that p[re]sently[78] upon the sight hereof he went to call Co[m]panye.

Munnery probably could not believe his young eyes, so perhaps rather foolishly called his employer, Joan Ewin.

---

[76] John Cox was landlord of the White Lion at Bramber at the time of his death in 1624.

[77] J. S. Cockburn, (ed.), *Calendar of Assize Records: Sussex Indictments, Elizabeth I*, (HMSO, 1973), 145, 153, 230, 284, 324.

[78] Presently = immediately

Joane Ewin, the wief of John Ewin, saith that being called by her s[er]vant William Munnerye, upon this report of the mare, she came to the stable, but sawe noe more but a yonge man, whom she now heares Called Thom[a]s Starke, standing w[i]th his back towardes a gray mare, w[i]th his handes something busied about his breeches before him. And more she cannot depose.

Now came the final nail in Starke's coffin – one of the parish officers, probably the town constable, was called.

Richard Constable of Steyning, upon this rumour com[m]ing downe to the stable, amongest others, he saw the haire of the Buttockes of a gray mare rased up, and a great deale of haire of the same Couler sticking upon the Jerkin and hose of the said yonge man called Thom[a]s Starke.[79]

Here the document ends, and here, also, ends the sad tale of Thomas Starke. He had acted foolishly, excited by the sexual ardour of the mare and stallion in the inn yard. Carried away by the moment, he signed his own death warrant. It is certain that the death penalty would have been given. He may have died in gaol, as happened to many prisoners, but the documents are silent.

Documentary research, which may seem so dull and dusty to some, opens a brief window on past lives, and, in this case, probably a death.

---

[79] WSRO, QSR, W5/4/64

Forgetting Thomas Starke and the grey mare, make your way along to Church Street, but pause momentarily at the corner opposite the White Horse, and look at across the road.

Fig. 39. The White Horse Inn.

The range with the Horsham stone roof was built c.1500. It was the kitchen of the inn in the 1920s. The former stables are hidden, but the old coach house can be seen behind the parasols.

The main part of the inn, which fronted the road, burnt down in March 1949. It is hard now to imagine the large building that imposed itself on this part of the town.

69

Fig. 40. Looking up Church Street from the Stone House on the corner of the High Street (no.21) and Sheep Pen Lane (formerly White Horse Lane), to Steyning Grammar School.

The white house on the left of the photograph is 2 Church Street formerly called Osborne House. It was the Office of the Registrar for births, marriages and deaths for a large area, the former Steyning Union. This included Hove, where Irishman Charles Stewart Parnell (1846-1891), former President of the Irish Nationalist Party, and his mistress, divorcée Kitty O'Shea, were living.

They married in Steyning on 26th June 1891, only three months before Parnell's death in Brighton. His body was taken to Ireland for burial,

70

but Kitty lived on for another thirty years and is buried in Littlehampton churchyard. Parnell was only forty-five years old when he died, and had fought hard and long for Irish Home Rule.

The scandal of the divorce and then the marriage meant that all Parnell's hopes for Irish nationalism and home rule were dashed, as it split the Irish Party and he lost the support of Mr. Gladstone, the Prime Minister. Local resident Frank Duke saw their carriage and pair outside the house, waiting to take them back to Hove.[80]

Fig. 41. The Blue Plaque at 2 Church Street, recording the marriage of Charles Stewart Parnell to Kitty O'Shea.

---

[80] Read more about this in I. Ivatt, 'Charles Stewart Parnell, 1846-1891', in *A Steyning Connection: Ten lives spanning 350 years,* (2001), 25-30; F. Duke & E. W. Cox, *In and Around Steyning: A Historical Survey Made in 1953,* (1954), 4

Walk along Church Street and just past the Grammar School, opposite the Norfolk Arms with its fine internal timber-framing, turn to the right down School Lane and so back to the Community Centre car park where this scandalous walk or reading tour began.

Fig. 42. The Norfolk Arms, Church Street.
School Lane, leading to the Community Centre, is opposite.

So, before leaving Steyning's past, perhaps we should again consider whether yesterday's scandal is today's entertainment? Perhaps we should all pause for thought and determine that our own behaviour will not cause a smile, a tear, horror or disgust, to Steyning inhabitants four hundred years hence. But would we worry if it did...?

Fig. 43. Steyning's Memorial Playing Fields
and the South Downs beyond.
Chanctonbury Ring is on the far right of the photograph.

*The poetry of history lies in the quasi-miraculous fact that once, on this earth, once, on this familiar spot of ground, walked other men and women, as actual as we are today, thinking their own thoughts, swayed by their own passions, but now all gone, one generation vanishing after another, gone as utterly as we ourselves shall shortly be gone, like ghosts at cock-crow.*[81]

---

[81] G. M. Trevlyan, An Autobiography and Other Essays, (1949), 13.

# BIBLIOGRAPHY

Primary Sources

West Sussex Record Office, PAR, 183/2/20, 22, 23, Steyning Parish Registers 1565-1652, 1755-1824, 1825-1872; EP1/23/5 Register of Churchwardens' Presentments, 1571-1682; Wiston MS, 5591, Map of Wiston and Steyning, 1639, by Henrie Bigg; QSR, W5/4/64, Session Roll, Sussex, July 1610, the information of John Balcombe

Primary Printed Sources

Cockburn, J. S., (ed.), *Calendar of Assize Records: Sussex Indictments, Elizabeth I,* (HMSO, 1973)
Hunnisett, R. F., (ed.), 'Sussex Coroners' Inquests 1485-1558', **Sussex Record Society** (hereafter **SRS**), **74,** (1984-85); *Sussex Coroners' Inquests 1603-1688,* (Public Record Office, 1998)
Redwood, B. C., 'Quarter Sessions Order Book, 1642-1649', **SRS, 54,** (1954)
Vaisey, D., (ed.), The Diary of Thomas Turner 1754-1765, (1994 edn)

Secondary Sources

Beckett, A., *Spirit of the Downs,* (1909)
Brabant, F. G., *Rambles in Sussex,* (1922, 2nd edn)
Calder-Marshall, A., *The Magic of My Youth,* (1951)
Davis, D., *History of Shopping,* (1966)
Duke, F., & Cox, E. W., *In and Around Steyning: A Historical Survey Made in 1953,* (1954)
Gosse, P., *Go To The Country,* (1935)
Greenwood, J., *The Posts of Sussex: The Chichester Branch 1250-1840,* (1973)
Grigg, C. A., *Memories of Steyning,* (1967)
Hey, D., (ed.), *The Oxford Companion to Local and Family History,* (1999 reprint)
Ivatt, I., *A Steyning Connection: Ten lives spanning 350 years,* (2001); The Race, (2003)
Jennings, L. *Rambles Among the Hills,* (1880)
Lucas, E. V., *Highways and Byways in Sussex,* (1904)
Maddox, B., *George's Ghosts: A New Life of W. B. Yeats,* (1999)
Neale, K., *Victorian Horsham: The Diary of Henry Michell 1809-1874,* (1975)

Neuburg, V. E., *Vickybird: A Memoir by his son,* (1983)
Oliver, R. *Out of the Woodshed. The Life of Stella Gibbons,* (1998)
Overton Fuller, J., *The Magical Dilemma of Victor Neuburg: Aleister Crowley's Magical Brother & Lover,* (2nd rev. edn, 2005)
Pennington, J., *St. Cuthman of Steyning: A Journey Through Time,* (1993 reprint); *The Chequer Inn, Steyning: Five centuries of innkeeping in a Sussex market town,* (1990)
Rutter, F., *Bertram Nicholls,* (1935)
Souhami, D., *Gluck 1895-1978: Her Biography,* (2001 edn)
Sutin, L., *Do What Thou Wilt: A Life of Aleister Crowley,* (2002)
Thurston Hopkins, R., *Sussex Pilgrimages,* (1927)
Trevelyan, G. M., *An Autobiography and Other Essays,* (1949)
Waugh, M., *Smuggling in Kent and Sussex 1700-1840,* (1998, rev. and updated)
Weir, A. & Jerman, J., *Images of Lust: Sexual Carvings on Medieval Churches,* (1986)
Williamson, T., *The Archaeology of Rabbit Warrens,* (2006)


Articles in Journals & Newsletters


Barron, W. A., 'Sidelights on Election Methods in the Eitheenth Century', **Sussex County Magazine, 24, no. 3,** (March 1950), 77-80
Blair, J., 'Saint Cuthman, Steyning and Bosham', **Sussex Archaeological Collections** (hereafter **SAC**), **135,** (1997), 173-92
Breach, W. Powell, 'Farnefold of Steyning', **SAC, 59,** (1918), 84-112
Heasman, W. A., & Pennington, J., 'Aunt Lizzie's Story – a description of Annington, Kingston Buci and Steyning in the Nineteenth Century', **West Sussex History, 73,** (Spring, 2004), 32-37
Lucas, P., 'Some Notes on the Early Sussex Quaker Registers, **SAC, 55,** (1912)
Pennington, J. 'An 'Image of Lust' on Steyning Church?', **SAC, 129,** (1991), 251-52; 'Documentary Evidence', in M. Bennell, 'New evidence for Saxo-Norman settlement at Chantry Green House, Steyning, West Sussex, 1989', **SAC, 138,** (2000), 226-27; 'Noysome savours and evell Ayers', **Steyning Museum Newsletter,** (December 2000); 'The Market-houses of Steyning', **SAC, 144,** (2006), 169-76; 'The Market Houses of Steyning', **Steyning Museum Newsletter,** (October 2005)
Sleight, J., 'The Poor Law in Steyning: II. Riot and a new regime', **West Sussex History, 22,** (May 1982), 19-24

Leaflets

*Equivalent Contemporary Values of the Pound: A Historical Series 1270-2001,* Bank of England, (2002)

Thesis

Pennington, J., 'The Inns and Taverns of Western Sussex, 1550-1700: A Regional Study of Their Architectural and Social History', (unpublished doctoral thesis, University of Southampton, 2003). Copies are available at Steyning Museum; the West Sussex Record Office, Chichester; Worthing Library Local History Studies Centre; Sussex Archaeological Society Library, Lewes; University Libraries of Chichester and Southampton; Inter-Library Loan (on microfilm)

## About the author...

Janet Pennington, born in Sussex, is a regional historian with a PhD in early-modern inn and tavern history. Her MA dissertation was about the history of Wiston House and the life of Sir Thomas Sherley (c.1542-1612), the owner and builder of the house, which is at Wiston, near Steyning in Sussex. In 1978 she joined the Wiston Estate Study Group, led by Roy Armstrong who founded the Weald & Downland Open Air Museum at Singleton; she was Secretary of the Group for many years while they recorded the agricultural buildings and farmhouses on the estate. She is a member of the Wealden Buildings Study Group which records and studies vernacular architecture in the south-east of England.

Janet was the archivist at Lancing College, an independent school in West Sussex, for eighteen years until she retired in 2004. She gives many illustrated talks throughout Sussex, particularly on pubs (inns, taverns and alehouses), Wiston House and a variety of other subjects, such as the ritual protection of the home. A list is available on request. With Joyce Sleight she has spent thirty years researching the history of Steyning – they have given many illustrated talks locally, and lead walks around the historic streets of the medieval town. They have both published numerous articles. Janet taught local history and palaeography for the Centre of Continuing Education at the University of Sussex for twenty years and undertakes house and pub histories in Sussex and Kent. She lives in Steyning with her husband and is always pleased to have enquiries from researchers by email or c/o Steyning Museum.